Plastic Handbags
Sculpture to Wear

**Revised 2nd edition
with updated prices**

Kate E. Dooner

Schiffer Publishing Ltd

4880 Lower Valley Road, Atglen, PA 19310 USA

Revised 2nd edition with updated prices
Copyright © 2005 by Schiffer Publishing Ltd.
Library of Congress Control Number: 2004114108

Designed by "Sue"
Type set in Liberty BT/Dutch801 Rm BT
ISBN: 0-7643-2213-3
Printed in China
1 2 3 4

Published by Schiffer Publishing Ltd.
4880 Lower Valley Road
Atglen, PA 19310
Phone: (610) 593-1777; Fax: (610) 593-2002
E-mail: Info@schifferbooks.com

For the largest selection of fine reference books on this and related subjects, please visit our web site at **www.schifferbooks.com** We are always looking for people to write books on new and related subjects. If you have an idea for a book please contact us at the above address.

This book may be purchased from the publisher.
Include $3.95 for shipping.
Please try your bookstore first.
You may write for a free catalog.

In Europe, Schiffer books are distributed by
Bushwood Books
6 Marksbury Ave.
Kew Gardens
Surrey TW9 4JF England
Phone: 44 (0) 20 8392-8585; Fax: 44 (0) 20 8392-9876
E-mail: info@bushwoodbooks.co.uk
Free postage in the U.K., Europe; air mail at cost.

Contents

Acknowledgements

Thank you to everyone who so readily offered their bags for photography including: Susann Spilkin; Dianne Rosenberg; Peggy Osborne; William Goldberg, Classics Illustrated; Larry Campbell, Radio Times; Kuku Antiques; Anne Hopkin, Anne Hopkin Flowers; Matthew Burkholz, Route 66 Antiques; Gary Franke and David Kratzer, Steppin' Out; Florence Geller, Piacente of Tarrytown, New York; and Roy Rover and Adrienne Lorber of Rover and Lorber, NYC. Also, to authors Robert Gottleib and Frank Maresca whose previous work *A Certain Style* helped focus attention on plastic handbags.

Those who have delved seriously into the research of plastic handbag manufacture realized there is not a great deal of historical information to research on these innovative bags; they should be enjoyed as functional sculpture to be worn and enjoyed from a wonderful and whimsical decade.

Chapter 1
The Age of Plastics Comes to Handbags

Imagine you are running out to the store, you grab your handbag; no, not the calf skin bag, the hard translucent Lucite bag in the shape of a birdcage with rhinestones trimming the edges. Not the typical pocketbook for your daily excursion? It certainly was for many women in the 1950s.

Plastics evolved during the decades which preceded the fifties. After celluloid was discovered in 1872, it was used primarily as an imitation material for natural plastics such as ivory and tortoise shell, for example. Next came Bakelite, a discovery of Belgian chemist Leo Backeland in 1905. Once the patents expired on Bakelite in 1927, all sorts of plastics pervaded the market and the use of colored plastics created a force in the American culture that would be hard to stop. Plastics were so ubiquitous by the 1950s, that its influence even touched women's handbags.

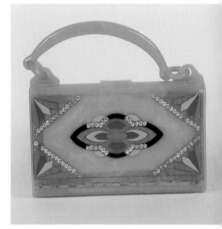

Tiny, Bakelite handbag with rhinestones, c. 1930s. 3.5" x 5" x 1". $475-525+ *Courtesy of Dianne Rosenberg.*

Plastics also enabled the emerging middle class to have items that were not available to them before. Handbags from the 1920s and 1930s made of natural plastics such as horn, tortoise shell and ivory were too expensive for the average woman. With the advent of synthetic plastics, bags that appeared to be natural were more widely affordable. The 1930s and 1940s also produced Bakelite handbags. They provided a look that was radically different from the elegant frames and bags of Europe. Just before the Second World War, translucent plastics trademarked "Plexiglas" by the Rohm & Haas Co., and "Lucite" by Du Pont, brought plastics to the cutting edge. The post-World War II era was a time ignited by "the modern." It was the dawn of the plastic handbag and women's handbags would not be the same for at least a decade!

As industrial designers created a popular streamlined look in the 1930s, such as the telephone and other daily appliances, modern plastics became a part of everyday life. This cultural phenomenon did not stop with the mechanical however, but was carried into every sphere of American life, including fashion. People from the fifties were enthralled by the "modern" and plastic handbags looked just that, with geometric shapes and modern designs. Any woman with a plastic bag in their hand would fit the "populuxe" mode.

The synthetic plastic handbag was born when it was discovered that these innovative, clear plastics could provide a beautiful material that could be tinted for elegant effects. The boxy-shaped bag was then in fashion, and the

Ribbed grey plastic bag with clear plastic ornamenting the lid and sides. Stands on four clear ball feet. By Rialto. 5" x 7" x 4". $450-475 *Courtesy of Dianne Rosenberg.*

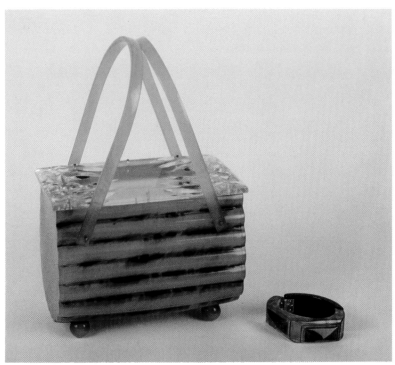

Ribbed sides with clear carved top, by Llewellyn. 5.5" x 7" x 4". $450-475 *Courtesy of Dianne Rosenberg.*

new material was perfect to meet the demand. "Acetate" was also a new plastic used by the fashion industry, and was stained and given a high polish to simulate tortoise shell. All sorts of decorations were added, to the delight of the consumer. Those looking for a sleek, classy, yet fun-filled alternative to leather and cloth covered handbags found it in the plastic bag. A craze "took off" as the bags were admired, not for their imitative value, but for their own identity as a novel plastic product.

The major manufacturers in the late 1940s and through the 1950s were small companies run by independent people with their eyes on the "popular" styles. These included: Myles Originals, Gilli Originals, Wilardy Originals, Rialto, Tyrolean Inc., Llewellyn Inc., Dorset-Rex, Charles S. Kahn, Maxim, Majestic, Miami and Florida Handbags.

Each manufacturer developed its own designs. Tyrolean, for instance, often trimmed its bags with a metal filigree. Wilardy manufactured the dressiest and most expensive bags. Llewellyn, whose trademark was the Lewsid Jewel, often lined its bags in silk. As you look through each section of this book, organized by manufacturer, you will notice the distinct style of each company, and you will also recognize the imitation that went on between them. The two bags pictured, for instance, are a perfect example of flattery. Who was being flattered, however, is uncertain. Rialto or Llewellyn?

The bags were lively and eccentric and epitomized America in the 1950s. But they were also well made. Many of the bags had clear, plastic lids with common motifs carved into them. These were hand-carved and then hand-processed on machines. Other bags came with kits enabling the customer to decorate the bags with shells, glitter or other imaginative materials.

The bags were also unique in that they were worn by almost every age group and every type of woman, from the teeny-bopper to the sophisticated lady. They were oftentimes advertised as "resort wear" bags as well, most being made in Miami and New York.

Eventually, the boxy bags became cumbersome and the madness for the eccentric began to fade as the bags became more and more specialized. As each manufacturer tried to out-do the other and provide a new design, odd shapes and ornaments constrained the bags as they became too eccentric for everyday use. Bags in the shapes of pagodas, bird cages, beehives, even coffins became too eccentric in the late fifties, and the novelty was beginning to wear off.

Another factor which aided in the demise of the plastic handbag at the end of the 1950s was the use of imitation bags by competitive new companies. The original plastic handbag manufacturers mentioned above were based in New York and Miami. As interest in the handbags rose, the bags were made by a large number of companies, from all over. As is often the case, the imitations were made with a flimsier plastic, less carefully, and they sold at much lower prices. These inexpensive bags were made from injection molds rather than parts that were assembled by hand.

Women no longer would pay fifty dollars for a hand-made bag that looked outwardly like a three dollar copy bag from an injection mold. When the idea of plastic was no longer new and in vogue, the style-conscious woman of the late fifties could no longer be seen wearing a plastic handbag. Many avid collectors say they can discern a cheap model from a better bag, either by a thinner plastic or by the catch.

The emergence of the so-called "mass culture" brought with it the downfall of plastics, which soon transformed from a 'classy' material, into a 'cheap' one that could be had by all. Women soon turned their tastes once again toward traditional materials and European-made handbags. Also, the discovery of vinyl and other pliable substances which could hold more, caused women to turn away from the boxy plastic bags.

These original plastic handbags have become a collector's craze. To many, these bags have an aesthetic value displayed through their extraordinary shapes and adornments of faux pearls, rhinestones, stars, stickers, shells, and even flowers, which give them an appeal that transcends time. These bags are unique, fun and completely contradictory to traditional standards. As awkward as they may be, with their boxy, fixed shapes, often not having enough space inside to hold all a woman would want to carry, they are definitely interesting. It seems people either love them or hate them.

The women who carried these bags in the fifties had no idea what their bags would be worth three decades later. Paying fifty dollars in the 1950s was an exorbitant rate in those days, but the value has risen in the '90s among collectors. Many people find an old plastic bag of their mother's or

Late 1940s, ivory-colored pearlized plastic bag by Simplex. This picture shows the back of the bag (front clasp is missing). 5.5" x 7". $375-425 *Courtesy of Classics Illustrated, William Goldberg.*

their own, perhaps, in the attic. Although it may look different, eccentric, even outrageous today, many people will pay well to own one.

Almost all of the bags made by the top-of-the-line manufacturers are marked on the inside of the bag, however, oftentimes these labels are lost and identification cannot be accurate. By the early 1950s when the bags were in full stride, other companies made the bags and did not provide a label. It is therefore difficult to differentiate whether a bag simply never had a label, or was a major designer bag and the label was lost.

Care and cleaning

"Shell colors which are acetate have greater resiliency and will take more 'hard knocks.' Lucite is fragile, and once dropped is usually gone. If your store is in a warm climate, it is not advisable to display shell bags in a window for too long a time. Overexposure to strong sunlight while in a stationary position will cause bags to fade. Polish smooth bags with glass wax to maintain their luster, or clean them by wiping with a damp cloth. You can, however, assure your customers that with normal care these plastic bags will give long and satisfactory service."

From a 1951 article in *Handbags and Accessories*, the handbag industry's trade magazine.

Chapter 2
Llewellyn Inc.

In 1951, Jewel Plastic Corp. and Fre-Mor Manufacturing Corp. merged to create Llewellyn, Inc. and the Llewellyn plastic bag was formed. Jewel Plastic Corp. was known for its carryalls and frames while Fre-Mor was known for handbags, particularly its beaded bags. Llewellyn Inc. was formed to design and produce plastic handbags and their trademark was Lewsid Jewel by Llewellyn. The company operated from Madison Avenue in New York City.

The Llewellyn line consisted of "jeweled and tailored, lined and unlined carryalls in unbreakable shell as well as crystal and topaz lucites. In addition to plastic boxes, there is a complete assortment of well styled leather bags, many trimmed with shell ornaments or 24k gold plated frames." (Sept. 1951 Handbags and Accessories). Morry Edelstein later went on to head Miami Handbags to which he added another line, Patricia of Miami.

Brown basket weave bag initialed O.S.M. Marked "Lewsid Jewel by Llewellyn". 5.5" x 5.5". $450-485 *Courtesy of Radio Times.*

Tortoise plastic bag by Llewellyn Inc. 7.75" x 5". $425-485 *Courtesy of Radio Times.*

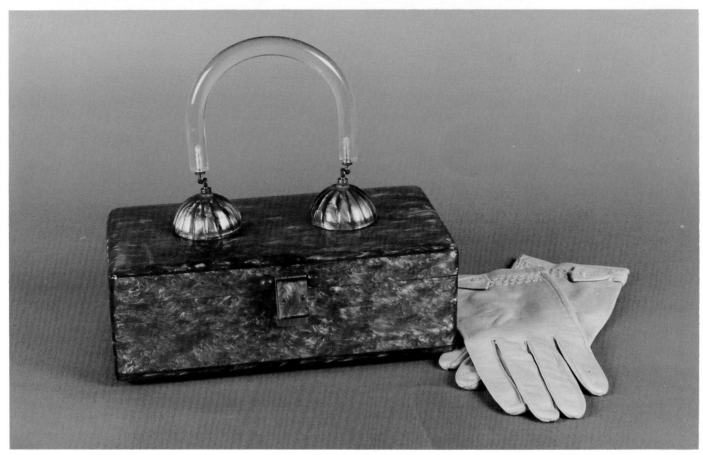

Grey bag with "cones" between the handle and purse. Lewsid Jewel by Llewellyn. 3" x 8.5" x 4.5". $350-425 *Courtesy of Susann Spilkin.*

Two clear plastic bags decorated with rhinestones. Left: unmarked, 8" x 4.25". $375-425 Right: clear with large faceted "jewels" surrounded by rhinestones, marked Llewellyn Inc., 7" x 3.5". $400-475+ *Courtesy of Radio Times.*

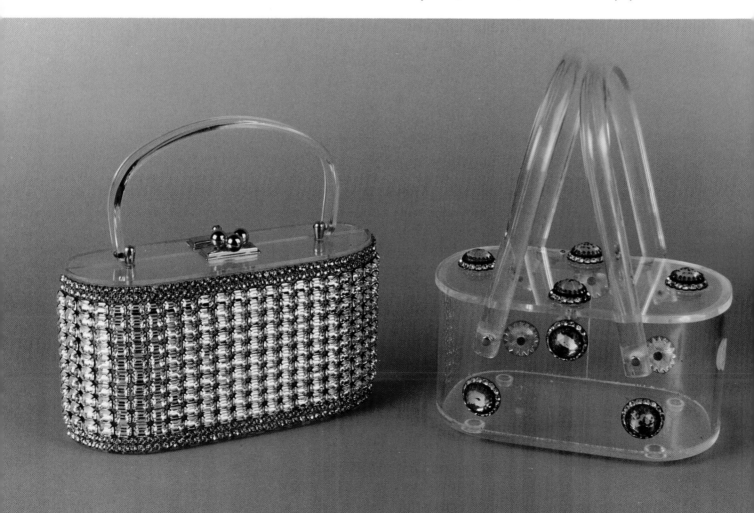

A black and a white plastic bag, each by Lewsid Jewel by Llewellyn. Both 7.5" x 6.75". $425-475 *Courtesy of Radio Times.*

Brown scalloped Lewsid Jewel by Llewellyn. 7" x 9.5" x 3". $425-475 *Courtesy of Dianne Rosenberg.*

A clear bag with greenish threads. By Llewellyn Inc. 4" x 7" x 4". $375-425 *Courtesy of Dianne Rosenberg.*

Brown rope borders this mock tortoise shell bag of plastic. Made by Llewellyn. 4.5" x 7" x 5". $375-450 *Courtesy of Dianne Rosenberg.*

Square tortoise shell bag with gold trim and two similar handles. Marked Lewsid Jewel TM, NYC by Llewellyn Inc. 8.5" w. x 6.75" h. $425-450 *Courtesy of Kuku Antiques.*

Two brown plastic bags. Left: scalloped front by Wilardy, 8.25" x 6.25". $425-475 Right: clear lid with rhinestones; Llewellyn; 9" x 2.75". $375-425 *Courtesy of Radio Times.*

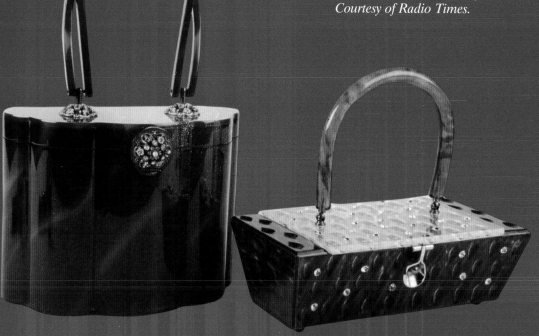

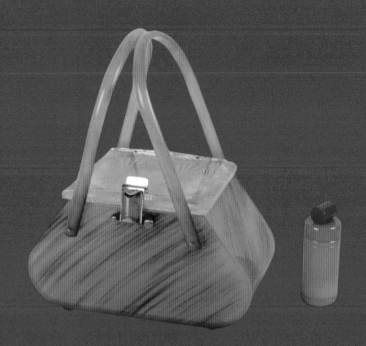

Llewellyn bag, the amber cut top displays a Deco pattern. 4.5" x 7" x 4". $425-475 *Courtesy of Susann Spilkin.*

The same bag in two different colors. Both by Llewellyn Inc. 10" x 3.5". $475-550 *Courtesy of Radio Times.*

The "beehive" bag was advertised by Llewellyn in 1951, "Bees and flowers on engraved jeweled top. Our 'Honey-topped Beehive.' In shell, blond, and jet with crystal top." 5.5" x 6" x 4". $475-525 Also advertised earlier in the year by Jewel Plastics Corp., the predecessor to Llewellyn. *Courtesy of Dianne Rosenberg.*

Dark tortoise plastic, a Lewsid Jewel by Llewellyn. 9" x 7.5" x 3". $375-450 *Courtesy of Susann Spilkin.*

Clear plastic bag with brown trim. Llewellyn. 5.5" d. x 5" h. $450-525 *Courtesy of Radio Times.*

Two tortoise shell type plastic bags. Left bag marked Lewsid—Jewel by Llewellyn. $375-450 Right bag has a clear plastic lid, unmarked. 7" x 4.25". $325-350 *Courtesy of Radio Times.*

Two stylish Llewellyn bags with similar stepped up designs. 3" x 7.5" x 5.5". $375-450 *Courtesy of Susann Spilkin.*

Two grey plastic bags. Left: unmarked, 8.75" x 5.75". $325-350 Right: Llewellyn Inc., 7" x 6.5". $375-425 *Courtesy of Radio Times.*

Lewsid Jewel by Llewellyn. 5.5" x 6.5" x 5". $375-425 *Courtesy of Dianne Rosenberg.*

Dark grey bag in soft half circle
shape. Lewsid Jewel by Llewellyn
Inc. 8" x 5.5". $385-450 *Courtesy of
Radio Times.*

Left: Gilli Originals mother-of-
pearl colored plastic. 4.75" h. x
8.25" w. x 4.25" d. $375-425 Right:
unique elastic handle decorated
with white balls. Llewellyn, 6" x 5" x
6". $400-425 *Courtesy of Dianne
Rosenberg.*

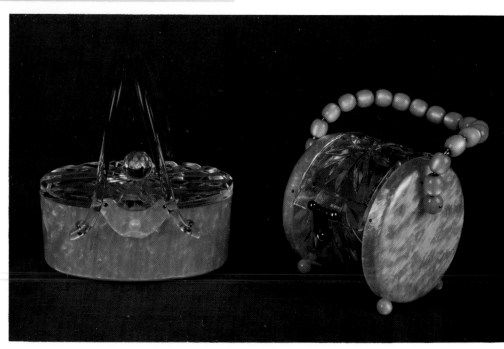

16

Three grey marble bags. Underneath, a briefcase type bag by Wilardy, 10" h. x 5" w. $425-475 On top, unmarked, 8" h. x 6" w. $325-350 Right, Llewellyn, 9.5" h. x 3.5" w. $375-425 *Courtesy of Radio Times.*

Brown plastic with brass initials, RSJ. Lewsid Jewel by Llewellyn. 7" x 5". $350-425 *Courtesy of Radio Times.*

Llewellyn grey box with clear top and two large four leaf clovers on lid. 4" x 6" x 4.5". $350-385 *Courtesy of Susann Spilkin.*

17

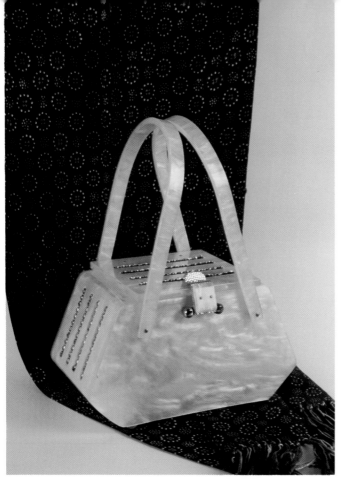

White bag decorated with lines of rhinestones. Llewellyn. 4.5" x 7.5" x 4". $375-400 *Courtesy of Susann Spilkin.*

Interesting design, Llewellyn. 6" x 12" x 4". $425-450 *Courtesy of Dianne Rosenberg.*

Lewsid Jewel by Llewellyn with initials on the front. 6.5" x 8.75" x 3". $350-375 *Courtesy of Dianne Rosenberg.*

All-clear cut bag by Llewellyn. 3.5" x 10" x 4". $350-375 *Courtesy of Dianne Rosenberg.*

Llewellyn Lewsid Jewel with unique clasp. 5.5" x 8" x 3". $375-425 *Courtesy of Dianne Rosenberg.*

Brown plastic with cloth lining inside. Although unmarked, it resembles a Llewellyn bag. 7.5" w. x 5.5" h. $385-450 *Courtesy of Radio Times.*

Tortoise shell color with fancy clasp as above, Lewsid Jewel for Llewellyn. 7.5" x 5.5" x 4". $375-425 *Courtesy of Susann Spilkin.*

Unique metalwork decorates this brown tortoise shell-colored plastic and the inside of the bag is lined with satin. It resembles a Llewellyn, however, it is not marked. 9.25" x 5" x 3". $325-350 *Courtesy of Susann Spilkin.*

Fre-Mor creation of amber suitcase style. 8.5" x 6.5" x 3". $350-375 *Courtesy of Susann Spilkin.*

Brown tortoise shell-colored plastic by Llewellyn. 4.5" x 6.5" x 4". $385-425 *Courtesy of Susann Spilkin.*

Grey scalloped, shell shaped bag by
Llewellyn. 9" w. x 4" h. x 4.5" d. $385-425
Courtesy of Susann Spilkin.

Unique purplish-blue plastic bag by Llewellyn. $385-425
Courtesy of Susann Spilkin.

Llewellyn, Inc. grey plastic handbag. 3.5" x 8". $350-375
Courtesy of Classics Illustrated, William Goldberg.

Chapter 3
Myles Originals

One of the few, original companies based in Miami, Florida, Myles created glamorous bags of all types and colors, many with a three ball clasp made of metal.

Beautiful black and grey marbleized plastic bag with angled sides and stacked layers. Three layers to the handles as well. Myles Original. 4" x 8" x 3.5". $375-425 *Courtesy of Susann Spilkin.*

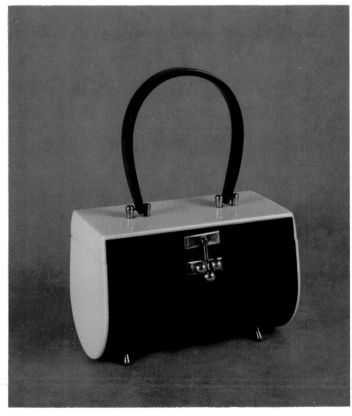

Unusual black with laminated white overtop. Myles Original. 5" x 7" x 4". $350-375 *Courtesy of Susann Spilkin.*

Another angled bag with accordion style layers all in black. Myles Original. 4" x 8" x 4". $325-375 *Courtesy of Dianne Rosenberg.*

Yellow with rhinestone clasp. Myles Originals of Miami. 7.5" x 6". $375-425 *Courtesy of Radio Times.*

Two yellow bags. Left: decorated with faux pearls, marked Weisner. 4" x 8" x 2.5". $350-375 Right: yellow marbled plastic with large rhinestones on top and small rhinestones surrounding the base. Myles Original. 4.5" x 4.5" x 4.5". $375-425+ *Courtesy of Susann Spilkin.*

23

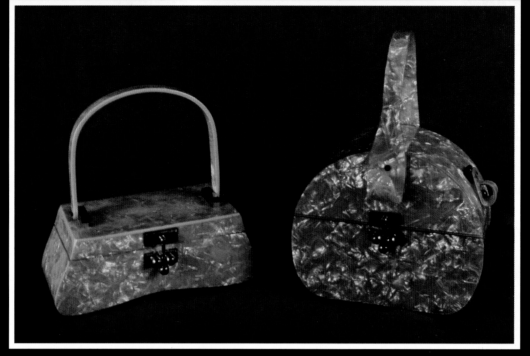

Two bags of a similar creamy marbled plastic. Left: inverted curve on the bottom, Myles Original, 3" x 8.5" x 4". $350-385 Right: unusual round curved shape with two compartments, one opening in front middle, the other on top, unmarked. 7" x 7.5" x 3.5". $325-350 *Courtesy of Susann Spilkin.*

Chapter 4
Gilli Originals

Owned by Associated Plastics, Gilli manufactured its bags in New York. Gilli bags were often decorated with gold or silver threads throughout the body, so typical of the fifties, or they carried solid, sleek looking bags.

A grey Gilli Original of New York. $350-375 *Courtesy of Anne Hopkin.*

Grey with gold threads common for a Gilli Originals bag. 8" x 6" x 3.5". $385-400 *Courtesy of Dianne Rosenberg.*

Another grey bag with gold threads and clear cut lid and handle. Gilli Originals. 5" x 9" x 3". $375-425 *Courtesy of Susann Spilkin.*

Pale yellow marbleized plastic with gold threads decorate this Gilli Originals bag. Clear ball sits on lid with rope style handles. 4" x 8.5" x 4.5". $375-425 *Courtesy of Susann Spilkin.*

Smaller grey Gilli Originals bag with clear cut lid and clear handle. 3.5" x 9" x 4". $350-400 *Courtesy of Dianne Rosenberg.*

Pretty caramel color plastic bag with two compartments. Gilli Originals, N.Y. $350-400 *Courtesy of Susann Spilkin.*

Left: elegant black plastic bag with gold clasp and decoration, 7.5" x 3.75". $350-375 Right: brown oval plastic bag with bow shaped handle, Gilli Originals, NY, 8" w. x 3.75" h. $375-400 *Courtesy of Route 66.*

Two ice box-style plastic bags in gold and silver each with a clear handle. Left: 6.5" x 7.5". Right: Gilli Originals, New York, 6.75" x 6.25". $375-425 ea. *Courtesy of Radio Times.*

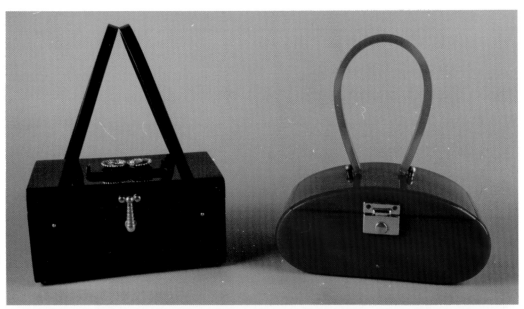

Two grey marble and confetti plastic bags by Gilli Originals, NY. Each has a clear decorated plastic lid and handle. Left, 7.5" w. x 5.5" h. Right, 9" w. x 5" h. $375-425 ea. *Courtesy of Radio Times.*

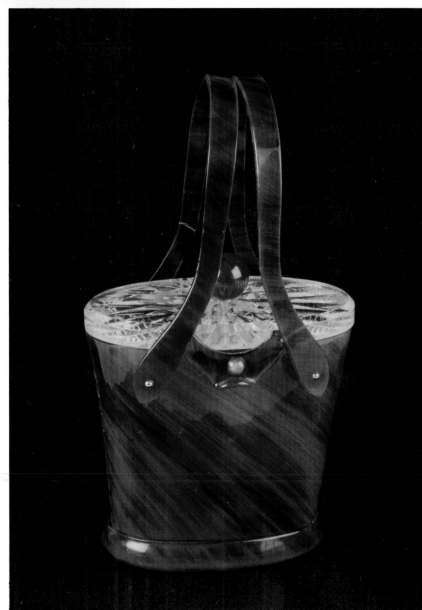

Brown swirled plastic with clear top. Gilli Original, NY. 8" x 7". $350-385 *Courtesy of Radio Times.*

Chapter 5
Tyrolean Inc.

Tyrolean was another manufacturer based in New York. The company's bags had a distinct design, often using a metal filigree to decorate the body or the lid of the bag.

Left: Grey bag with mesh insert in front with rhinestones, Tyrolean, 4" x 7.5" x 2" $400-450+,. Right: White bag with half circle shape with clover leaf mesh inserts with rhinestones, Tyrolean, 6" x 7" x 3". $425-475+ *Courtesy of Susann Spilkin.*

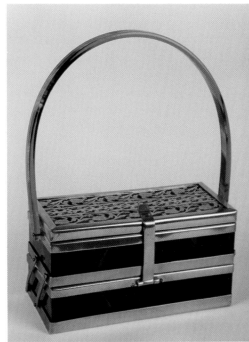

Left: Round tortoise shell-colored plastic with gold filigree trim on each side, Tyrolean, 4" x 8" x 4". Right: Box shaped bag of a similar style, Tyrolean, 4.5" x 6" x 4". $350-400 ea. *Courtesy of Dianne Rosenberg.*

Accordion type tortoise plastic bag with silver lid and trim, Tyrolean. Shown open and closed. 3.5" x 6.5" x 3.5". $350-375 *Courtesy of Dianne Rosenberg.*

Brown plastic bordered with gold meshwork detail, Tyrolean. $350-400 *Courtesy of Radio Times.*

Two brown handbags. On the left, brass and pierced metal enhance the plastic design. Tyrolean, NY. 7" w. x 4.5" h. $350-400 On the right, the oval shape reinforces the soft feel of the plastic with metal only used in the handle, unmarked. 7.25" x 4.5". $250-275 *Courtesy of Route 66.*

Left: brown plastic with brass trim and screening; made by Tyrolean, 5.25". $350-400 Right: rectangular brown bag with clear cut lid and handle, unmarked, 7.25" x 3". $275-325 *Courtesy of Radio Times.*

Two plastic handbags. Left: clear vinyl with stitched black and white ribbons sandwiched inside, by Tyrolean, New York. $200-225 Right: dark brown hard plastic bag with brass framed pierced holes, maker unknown. $185-200 *Courtesy of Steppin' Out.*

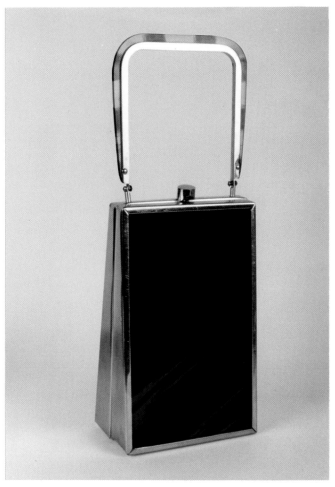

The metal frame contrasts well with this dark brown plastic by Tyrolean. 9" x 5" x 3". $350-375 *Courtesy of Dianne Rosenberg.*

White bag with tapered sides and metal frame typical of Tyrolean style, Tyrolean. 4" x 7.5" x 4.5". $325-375 *Courtesy of Susann Spilkin.*

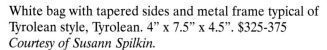

Clear plastic bag with cloth lining. Tyrolean. 5" x 8" x 3". $325-375 *Courtesy of Dianne Rosenberg.*

Another white bag with silver mesh and trim. Maker uncertain yet similar to the Tyrolean style. 5.5" x 5" w. $275-350 *Courtesy of Route 66.*

Plastic handbag with 24K gold plated top, by Tyrolean, c.1956. 3.5" x 6.25". $350-400 *Courtesy of Classics Illustrated, William Goldberg.*

Beautiful capio shell bag by Tyrolean, NY. 7" w. x 10" h. $450-525 *Courtesy of Route 66.*

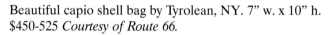

Another shell bag with silver trim by Tyrolean. 8" x 7". $450-525 *Courtesy of Susann Spilkin.*

33

Chapter 6
Rialto

Rialto advertised in August of 1954 its wafer shape shell carryall as a new silhouette for fall with twin swivel handles. The lid was of a heavy carved Lucite. This was one bag from their new "flat" look series. Rialto definitely was one of the more elegant manufacturers.

Left: Clear bag with optical daisies and rhinestones and a reverse cut button clasp, Rialto Originals, 4" x 8.5" x 4". $375-400 Right: all clear bag with thick faceted lid, made by Maxim, 6.5" x 6" x 3.5". $325-375 *Courtesy of Susann Spilkin.*

Brown plastic handbag with clear cut lid. Rialto Originals. 7.5" x 4.5" x 4". $350-375 *Courtesy of Susann Spilkin.*

Two brown plastic bags by Rialto. Left: heart leaf pattern in lid, 4" x 8" x 3.5". Right: clear cut lid, 5.5" x 6" x 4". $325-375 ea. *Courtesy of Susann Spilkin.*

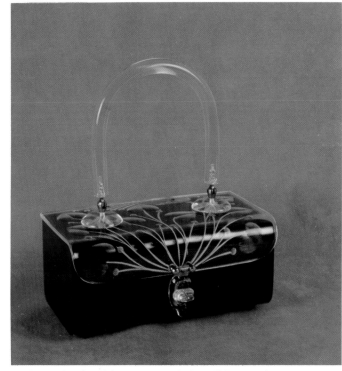

Black plastic with an unusual clear lid curved to meet the body of the bag. Once again the heart leaf pattern is seen in the lid. Rialto. 3.5" x 7.5" x 4". $350-425 *Courtesy of Susann Spilkin.*

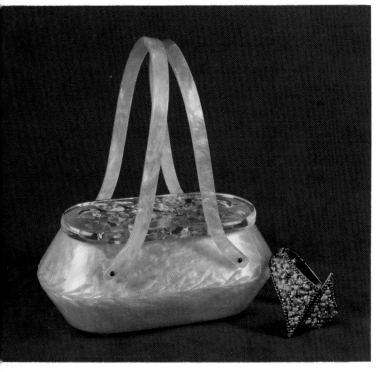

The same bag as the bag on the left; in a white marbleized plastic. Rialto, 9" x 4" x 5". $325-375 *Courtesy of Susann Spilkin.*

Standing on four clear ball feet, a white bag with clear cut top by Rialto. 4" x 7" x 3.5". $375-425 *Courtesy of Susann Spilkin.*

Grey plastic with trimmed scalloped decoration on the front. Rialto. 8" x 3" x 3.75". $400-450 *Courtesy of Susann Spilkin.*

Black and gold designed plastic with chain and plastic handle. Rialto. 7.5" x 8.5" x 3.75". $325-375 *Courtesy of Dianne Rosenberg.*

White bag with plastic on the lid and metal decoration. Rialto. 3.5" x 7.5" x 4". $400-450 *Courtesy of Susann Spilkin.*

Long brown plastic bag looks like a log. Rialto. 9.5" x 3.75" x 3.5". $325-375 *Courtesy of Susann Spilkin.*

White plastic with rhinestones and plastic decorating the front. Rialto. 7" x 7" x 2". $375-425 *Courtesy of Dianne Rosenberg.*

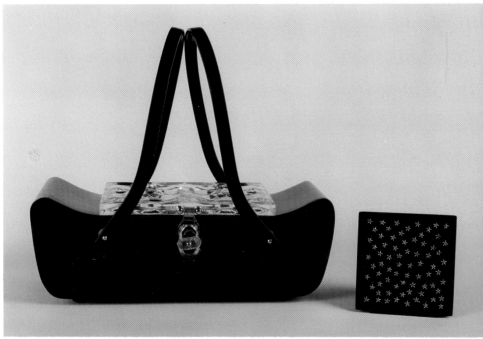

Elongated pagoda shaped bag showing an Oriental influence. Rialto. 3" x 9.5" x 4". $375-425 *Courtesy of Susann Spilkin.*

Interesting swirled, pearlized plastic with fancy beadworked lid. Rialto. 4.5" x 7.5" x 5.5". $450-525 *Courtesy of Dianne Rosenberg.*

Similar color to the bag above, this bag has a clear lid. Rialto. 9" x 6" x 3.5". $325-375 *Courtesy of Susann Spilkin.*

Two decorative plastic handbags. Left: light grey plastic with floral appliqué and white beads, 8.25" x 3.5". Right: light grey pearl bag bordered with flowers, made by Rialto, NY. 6.25" x 5.25". $275-350+ ea. *Courtesy of Route 66.*

Brown oval tortoise shell plastic with clear cut design for the lid. Marked "Rialto Original, NY." 10" x 3.25". $325-375 *Courtesy of Kuku Antiques.*

Left: grey plastic handbag by Rialto. 7" x 6". $300-350 Right: maker uncertain, 8" x 8". $325-375 *Courtesy of Radio Times.*

Pretty white marbleized bag with a heavy clear cut lid. Rialto Originals, NY. 4" x 7" x 5". $325-375 *Courtesy of Susann Spilkin.*

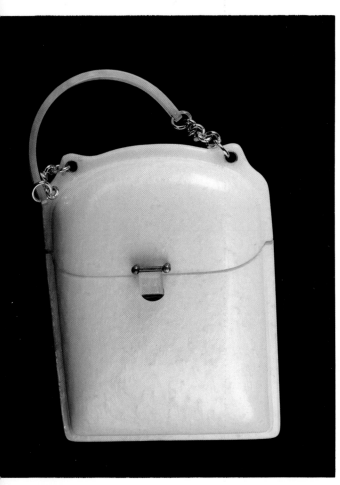

White envelope bag with chain and solid handles. Rialto, NY. 7.75" x 10". $300-350 *Courtesy of Radio Times.*

White plastic with clear cut front lid and handles. Made by Rialto, NY. 6.75" x 7.25". $375-400 *Courtesy of Radio Times.*

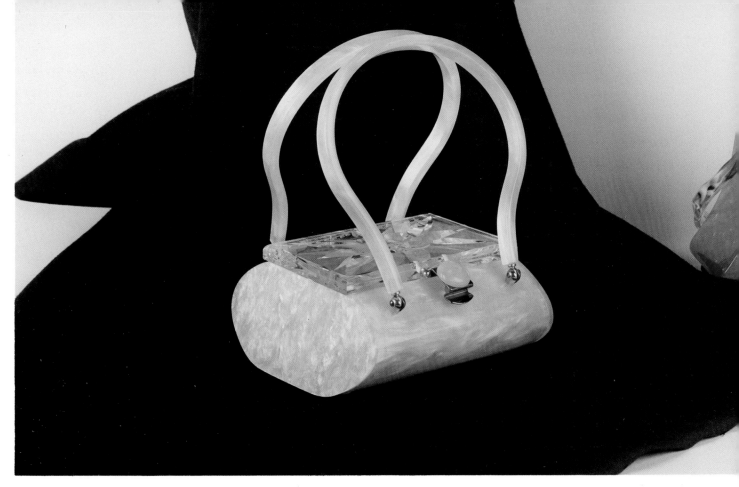

White marbled plastic handbag with clear decorative plastic lid. The handles have a pretty curve. Marked Rialto, NY. 3" x 6.5". $425-485 *Courtesy of Radio Times.*

Left: white plastic bag with clear lid, made by Rialto, NY. 7" x 4.25". $450-485 Right: white square bag with compact and lipstick in front. Made by Elgin American Carryall. Division of Illinois Watch Case Co., Elgin, Il. 4.75" x 3.75". $375-425 *Courtesy of Radio Times.*

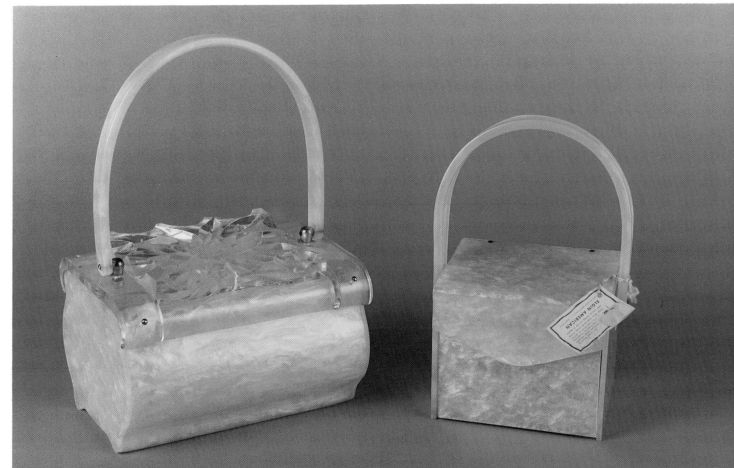

Chapter 7
Wilardy Originals

Wilardy Originals was based in the New York area. They were a big name when it came to hard, plastic handbags in the 1950s, often using solid colors for their bags.

Wilardy label advertising the bag for "fashion wise women."

This plastic bag has a curve in the bag giving it a unique shape. The metalwork and rhinestone decoration on the clasp and lid make the bag more formal. Wilardy. 6.5" x 7.5" x 5". $450-525+ *Courtesy of Susann Spilkin.*

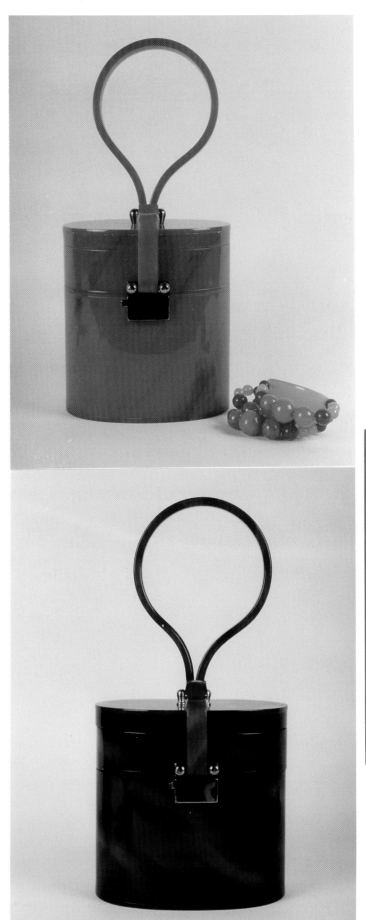

Grey bag with gold metal trim. Wilardy. 7.5" x 4.25" x 3". *Courtesy of Susann Spilkin.*

This Wilardy Original was advertised in 1951 as a "stardust" bag retailing for $13.50. "Gold lace and sparkles within Lucite makes 'Stardust'". This double decker bag with accordion bar hinge and self lock was advertised with a matching tiny carryall. 3.75" x 5.75" x 4.75". $350-400 *Courtesy of Dianne Rosenberg.*

Two Wilardy handbags of the same design but different color, 6" x 5.75" x 4". $385-450 *Courtesy of Dianne Rosenberg and Susann Spilkin.*

White marbleized plastic bag by Wilardy with two openings. 6" x 6.75" x 3.75". $425-475 *Courtesy of Dianne Rosenberg.*

Brown double envelope style bag by Wilardy. 6" x 5" x 3.5". $385-450 *Courtesy of Susann Spilkin.*

Navy plastic bag by Wilardy. 4.5" x 7.5" x 4.25". $350-375 *Courtesy of Dianne Rosenberg.*

Brown plastic Wilardy bag with metal clasp. 6" x 8" x 3.5". $350-385 *Courtesy of Dianne Rosenberg.*

Compact bag shown open. Wilardy Originals. 4" x 6.5" x 3". $450-500+ *Courtesy of Susann Spilkin.*

Elegant navy, straight-backed bag with filigree clasp and handle attachments. Wilardy. 4" x 10.5" x 4". $375-450 *Courtesy of Susann Spilkin.*

Same Wilardy bag as above in tan. $375-450 *Courtesy of Dianne Rosenberg.*

A very unusual and rare, iridescent bag by Wilardy. The colors change from blue to gold. $500-525+ *Courtesy of Susann Spilkin.*

Fancy detailed trim on this plastic bag with the large round clasp. Wilardy. 3.75" x 7" x 4". $450-525+ *Courtesy of Dianne Rosenberg.*

Wilardy bag with metal decoration on the clasp and handle attachments. 4.25" x 9" x 4.25". $425-450 *Courtesy of Dianne Rosenberg.*

This bag has slits in the sides of the handles and gold threads and decorations inlaid beneath the plastic to jazz it up a bit. Wilardy. 4" x 7" x 5". $375-425 *Courtesy of Dianne Rosenberg.*

White oval bag with rows of rhinestones. Wilardy. 3" x 8" x 4.5". $450-525+ *Courtesy of Susann Spilkin.*

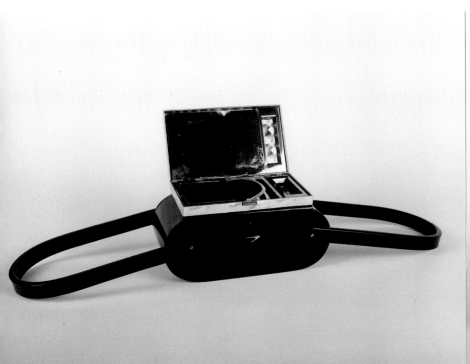

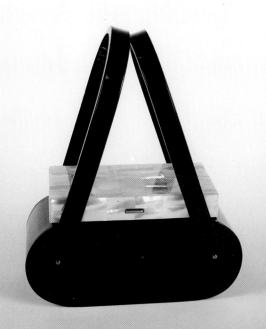

Compact bag by Wilardy, shown open and closed. 4" x 7" x 3". $425-500+ *Courtesy of Dianne Rosenberg.*

Fancy rhinestone-decorated bag by Wilardy with the original tag attached. 4.5" x 6.5" x 4". $500-550+ *Courtesy of Susann Spilkin.*

Black plastic with fancy trim by Wilardy. 3.5" x 8" x 5". $500-550+ *Courtesy of Dianne Rosenberg.*

Another set of fancy black bags by Wilardy. Left: 4" x 9". x 3". Right, 6" x 6" x 2". $500-550+ *Courtesy of Dianne Rosenberg.*

Navy blue bag with a unique rolled front. Wilardy. 7" x 4.25" x 5". $400-450 *Courtesy of Susann Spilkin.*

Tall, navy blue bag by Wilardy with elegant clasp. 6" x 6.75" x 3.75". $400-425 *Courtesy of Susann Spilkin.*

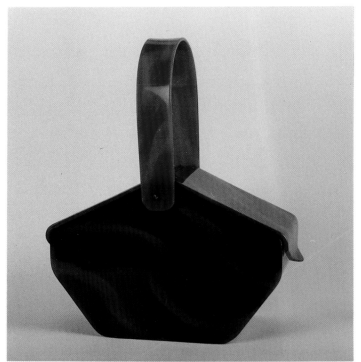

Subtle, smokey waves smooth out this plastic bag by Wilardy. 9.5" x 4.25" x 6". $375-425 *Courtesy of Susann Spilkin.*

Grey bag with twisted handle by Wilardy. 6" x 6" x 4". $375-425 *Courtesy of Susann Spilkin.*

A scalloped front body with a rhinestone decoration on the clasp and handle attachments. Wilardy. 6" x 8" x 4". $400-425 *Courtesy of Susann Spilkin.*

The same style bag in a light grey plastic with the twisted handle. Wilardy Original. 6" x 5.75". $400-450 *Courtesy of Radio Times.*

Left: this bag looks like it could be a fine leather bag. Sleek black plastic and twisted handle by Wilardy, 6". $375-425 Right: elegant octagonal white sparkled plastic with rhinestone border and clear lid, unmarked. $275-350 *Courtesy of Radio Times.*

50

White marbleized bag with silver metal decoration on the clasp and handle attachments. Wilardy. 4.5" x 11.5" x 3". $375-400 *Courtesy of Susann Spilkin.*

This bag is rare because of its color—red! Wilardy, 4.5" x 9" x 4". $475-525 *Courtesy of Susann Spilkin.*

Grey marbled plastic in scalloped shape. Wilardy. 6.25" x 5.5". $475-550 *Courtesy of Radio Times.*

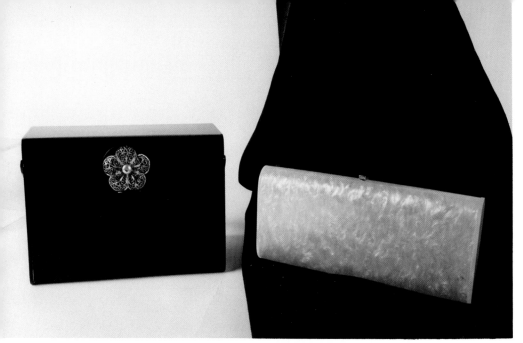

Two elegant evening bags in plastic! Left: solid black bag with an attractive gold floral clasp, Wilardy Original, 8.5" x 6". $325-375 Right: white clutch back with pretty nacre glaze, also a Wilardy Original, 9.25" x 4.25". $250-285 *Courtesy of Route 66.*

White plastic handbag with labels of cities decorating the bag, unmarked. 10" x 6.25". $275-425+ *Courtesy of Route 66.*

Dark blue plastic handbag, Wilardy Original. 5.75" x 3.75". $325-375 *Courtesy of Radio Times.*

Left: grey plastic, 8" x 7.5". $325-375 Right: white Wilardy Original with a catch by Presto Lock Co. 8.5" x 6.5". $350-400 *Courtesy of Route 66.*

Two "travel trunk" bags decorated with hand painted travel stickers in gold on the left and in rhinestones on the right. Advertised by Wilardy Originals in 1951. 9" x 4.5". $375-425+ ea. *Courtesy of Radio Times.*

Grey marble bag. A Wilardy Original. 6.25" x 9.5". $400-425 *Courtesy of Radio Times.*

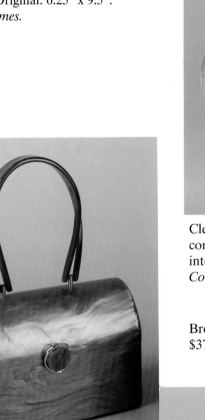

Clear with gold tulle and sparkles, Wilardy's 'Stardust'. A compact with powder, a comb, lipstick and a mirror fit into the top. Wilardy Original. 7" x 3.75". $450-525 *Courtesy of Radio Times.*

Brown "lunch pail" style plastic bag. Wilardy. 8.75" x 5.5". $375-425 *Courtesy of Radio Times.*

Left: small cream bag with a clear handle, unmarked. 11" x 3.75". $275-325 Right: brown slatted plastic bag by Wilardy. 9.75" x 4.75". $375-400 *Courtesy of Radio Times.*

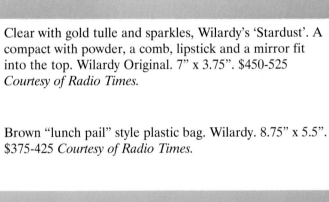

54

Chapter 8
Miami Handbags

Morty Edelstein, who was the "Mor" of Fre-Mor bags, later worked for Llewellen Inc. Still later, he headed Miami Handbags, in Miami, Florida. He added another line which was called Patricia of Miami, Patricia being his wife, Patricia Edelstein.

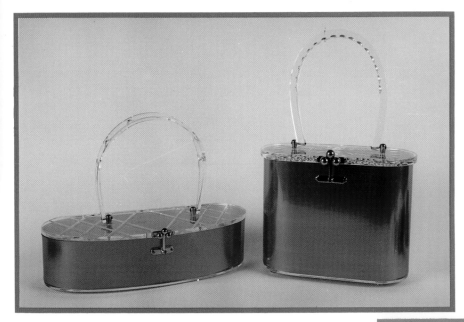

Left: Fuschia colored Florida Handbag. 3" x 10" x 4".
Right: Charles S. Kahn, 6.5" x 7.5" x 3.5". $400-450 ea.
Courtesy of Susann Spilkin.

White with speckles and clear cut lid and handle, Florida Handbags. 4.5" x 7.5" x 4.5". $425-450 *Courtesy of Susann Spilkin.*

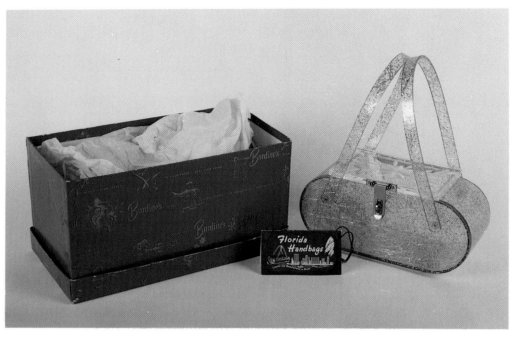

Clear bag with confetti and gold threads. Florida
Handbags with original Burdines gift box. 4" x 8" x 4".
$475-550 *Courtesy of Susann Spilkin.*

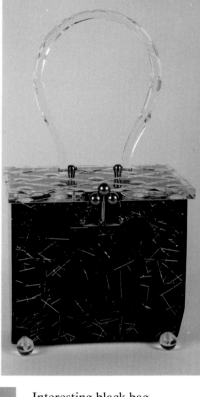

Interesting black bag
with gold speckles and
clear lid. Florida
Handbags. 5.75" x 6.5" x
4". $400-425 *Courtesy of
Dianne Rosenberg.*

Left: yellow rhinestones decorate the cut plastic pattern of
this bag, made by Florida Handbags, Miami, 7.5" x 3.5".
$400-450 Right: unique black lace designed across this
clear plastic bag, maker uncertain, 8" x 5". $375-425
Courtesy of Route 66.

Grey and gold speckles decorate this bag made by Florida Handbags, Miami. 8" x 4". $375-400 *Courtesy of Radio Times.*

Elegant grey marbled plastic handbag with clear cut plastic lid and handle. Label shows this bag is a Florida Handbag. 6" w. x 5.5" h. $400-475 *Courtesy of Route 66.*

Pink and white plastic bags with sparkles. Left: delicate pink made by Miami Handbags, 8" x 4". $475-525 Right: unmarked, 8" x 6". $275-350 *Courtesy of Radio Times.*

Grey '50s design with a clear cut lid and double handles. Florida Handbags, Miami. 10.25" x 3". $375-425 *Courtesy of Radio Times.*

"Confetti" plastic bag of gold and black speckles on white with clear lid and handle. Marked "Florida Handbags, Made in Miami." 6" x 7.75". $375-425 *Courtesy of Kuku Antiques.*

Pearlized white plastic bag with clear lid and handle. Marked "Florida Handbags, Made in Miami." 7.25" x 4.5". $425-475 *Courtesy of Kuku Antiques.*

Patricia of Miami

Greenish-yellow bag with gold threads throughout.
Filigree center and two openings by Patricia of Miami.
3.5" x 10.25" x 4". $475-525 *Courtesy of Susann Spilkin.*

The same bag by Patricia in a darker color. 3.5" x 10.25" x
4". *Courtesy of Dianne Rosenberg.*

Yet another version of the same bag by Patricia, shown
open and closed. $475-525 *Courtesy of Susann Spilkin.*

Another bag by Patricia with a long, narrow body. Reddish tortoise shell plastic. 3" x 12" x 4.5". $425-485 *Courtesy of Susann Spilkin.*

Unusual grey plastic bag with horizontal stripes. Made by Patricia of Miami. 8" x 6.5". $475-550+ *Courtesy of Radio Times.*

The plastic bag on the left is a typical Patricia of Miami handbag with gold thread laced throughout and the three buttoned clasp. 5" x 7" x 4". $350-425 Right: mink brown bag with clear top of large clear buttons filled with gold thread, unmarked. $275-350 *Courtesy of Susann Spilkin.*

Two plastic evening bags in black and gold. Left: unmarked but very unusual, 9" x 3.75". $375-450 Right: Patricia of Miami; 7.25" x 4.5". $375-425 *Courtesy of Radio Times.*

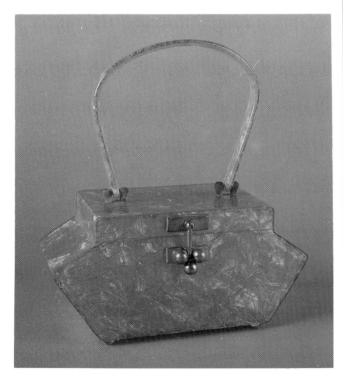

Chartreuse bag of a cute shape by Patricia of Miami and the same bag in grey with silver threads throughout. 8.25" x 4". Left photo: $450-525. Right photo: $375-425. Price difference is based on color. *Courtesy of Radio Times and Susann Spilkin.*

61

Clear plastic decorated with brown and gold by Patricia of Miami. 4" x 10" x 4.5". $375-425 *Courtesy of Dianne Rosenberg.*

Patricia of Miami bag. 5" x 8" x 3.5". $400-450 *Courtesy of Dianne Rosenberg.*

Very boxy, brown marbled plastic bag with clear lid. Patricia of Miami. 12" w. x 4" h. $400-450 *Courtesy of Radio Times.*

Unusual filigree and rhinestone combination decorate the front of this marbleized green and gold thread bag. Patricia of Miami. 5" x 9" x 3.5". $550-625+ *Courtesy of Susann Spilkin.*

"Ice bucket" style bag by Patricia of Miami. 6.5" x 8" x 4". $475-500+ *Courtesy of Dianne Rosenberg.*

Acetate bag of an unusual burgundy color with a clear cut lid. Patricia of Miami. 5" x 5.5" x 4". $375-425 *Courtesy of Susann Spilkin.*

Yellowish-green plastic with gold sparkles by Patricia of Miami. 3.5" x 8" x 3.5". $400-450 *Courtesy of Dianne Rosenberg.*

Two elegant rhinestone evening bags by Patricia of Miami. Left: 4" x 10" x 4". Right: 5" x 8" x 3.5". $500-575 ea. *Courtesy of Susann Spilkin.*

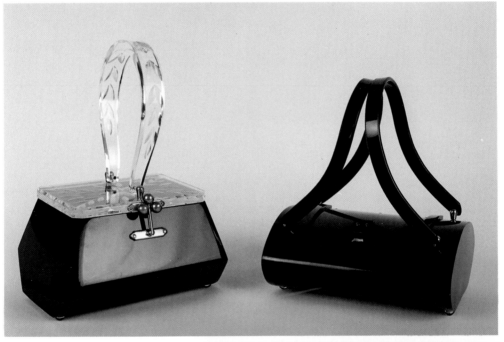

Two sleek black bags. Left: unmarked, clear cut lid, 4.5" x 7" x 5.75" $285-350; Right: Patricia of Miami, 2.75" x 7.25" x 5.75" $375-425. *Courtesy of Dianne Rosenberg.*

Greenish-yellow bag with gold threads, clear cut angled sides and a clear cut top. Patricia of Miami. 4" x 9" x 3.5". $275-425 *Courtesy of Susann Spilkin.*

Chapter 9
Charles S. Kahn

Charles S. Kahn was a Miami, Florida based manufacturer. Often the company's bags were a solid metallic color, often using a pink color.

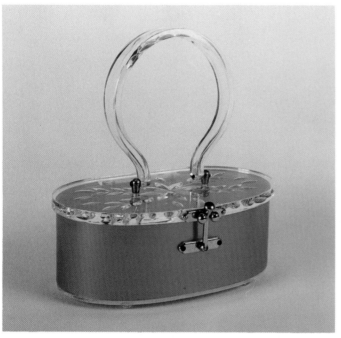

Metallic pink bag with clear cut lid and clear handle. Charles Kahn, Miami. 3" x 7.5" x 4". $350-400 *Courtesy of Susann Spilkin.*

The same bag with a clear metallic body. Charles Kahn, Miami. 3" x 7.5" x 4". $325-385 *Courtesy of Dianne Rosenberg.*

Rectangular form of the same bag. Charles Kahn, Miami. 3" x 7" x 3.5". $325-385 *Courtesy of Susann Spilkin.*

Round version of the same bag. Charles Kahn, Miami. 3" x 6.5" x 6". $375-450 *Courtesy of Susann Spilkin.*

Confetti gold on white plastic handbag with a clear cut lid and handle. Marked "Charles S. Kahn, Inc., Miami, Florida, U.S.A." 8.25" x 4.25". $375-400 *Courtesy of Kuku Antiques.*

Gold pieces decorate this white plastic bag shown with period glasses. Made by Charles S. Kahn, Inc., Miami. 8.25" x 3.75". $375-400 *Courtesy of Route 66.*

Chapter 10
Dorset-Rex

Dorset-Rex often combined metal with plastic in its plastic bags. A well-known Dorset-Rex bag among plastic handbag collectors is the metal basketweave bag.

Grey taupe plastic with gold mesh body and clear handle. Dorset-Rex. 7.75" x 3.5" x 5". $375-400 *Courtesy of Susann Spilkin.*

Basketweave of metal and black plastic. Dorset-Rex. 6.5" x 7" x 5". $350-425 *Courtesy of Dianne Rosenberg.*

Brass basketweave with tortoise plastic top and handle. Dorset-Rex, NY. 6.5" x 7" x 5". $350-425 *Courtesy of Susann Spilkin.*

Clear plastic decorated with flowers by Dorset-Rex of Fifth Ave., NY. 4" x 6" x 6". $375-425 *Courtesy of Dianne Rosenberg.*

Basket type bag typical of the Dorset-Rex style. Silver metal and black plastic. Dorset-Rex. 4.75" x 9.5" x 6". $450-500+ *Courtesy of Dianne Rosenberg.*

Barrel shaped tortoise plastic and gold overlay. Made by Dorset-Rex for Saks Fifth Ave. 4.5" x 7" x 4". $375-450 *Courtesy of Susann Spilkin and Dianne Rosenberg.*

Two elegant white plastic evening bags. Left: filigree decoration on lid, interesting shape with rounded bottom shown at back. Tyrolean, 5.5' x 6" x 2.5". $475-500 Right: mother-of-pearl box bag with gold trim. Dorset-Rex, 4" x 5" x 5". $425-475+ *Courtesy of Susann Spilkin.*

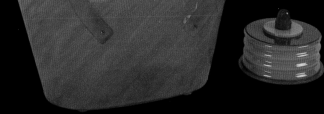

Light tortoise color in basket style with clear, amber top with jagged edge and ball clasp, Maxim. 4.5" x 8.5" x 4". $400-450 *Courtesy of Susann Spilkin.*

Tortoise shell color with heavy, clear, curved top by Maxim. 5.5" x 6" x 5". $400-450 *Courtesy of Susann Spilkin.*

Very unusual clear amber bag by Maxim. 3.5" x 8" x 4". $475-525 *Courtesy of Susann Spilkin.*

Black oval bag covered in pattern of black beading. Maxim for Saks Fifth Avenue. 3.5" x 8.5" x 4.5". $550-575+ *Courtesy of Susann Spilkin.*

Clear rectangular bag covered in a delightful black bead pattern. Maxim for Saks Fifth Avenue. 3.5" x 8" x 3.5". $500-550+ *Courtesy of Susann Spilkin.*

70

Lantern shape bag with a metal lid and a "tweedy" plastic body. Majestic. 5.5" x 5" x 4". $275-350 *Courtesy of Susann Spilkin.*

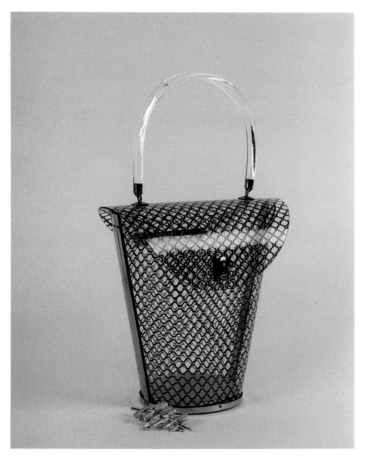

Tall bag with gold trim and lace pattern. Majestic. 6.25" x 3.25" x 4". $275-350 *Courtesy of Susann Spilkin.*

One thinks of glitter baskets when it comes to the Majestic plastic bags.

Tall bag with rounded envelope style lid. Majestic. 7.5" x 7" x 3". $275-350 *Courtesy of Susann Spilkin.*

Chapter 12
Various Manufacturers

Other companies were making the plastic bags but not exclusively. Therefore, their names were not as prominent in terms of the plastic bags. These include: Nelson Originals; Weisner; Koret; Vanity Fashions; and many others.

Tortoise color with fixed handle of amber with cut pattern, unmarked but same design as above right. Presto Lock Co. 4" x 7.75" x 4.5". $375-425 *Courtesy of Susann Spilkin.*

White bag of the same design with fixed handle and clear, cut handle and lid. Majestic. 4" x 7.5" x 4.5". $375-425 *Courtesy of Susann Spilkin.*

An amber plastic with gold metal body. Marked MW Handbag with original tag and card noting care for the bag. 8" x 3.25" x 4". $450-475 *Courtesy of Susann Spilkin.*

Plastic handbag with brown ribbed sides and single handle and molded yellow hinged lid, marked "A Cadillac Presentation, Made in USA," 7.75" x 4" d. $325-350 *Courtesy of Piacente, Tarrytown, NY.*

Plastic handbag with grey fluted base and handles and clear lid embellished with sea shells, pearls and coral, marked "Theresa Bag Co., Lyndhurst, NJ." 8" x 4". $275-300 *Courtesy of Piacente, Tarrytown, NY.*

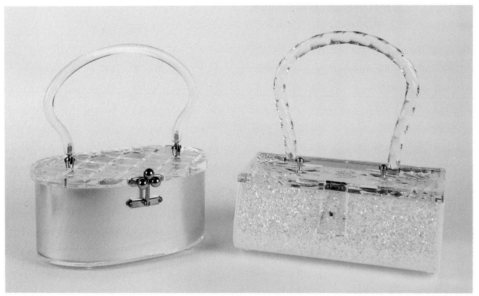

Left: Charles Kahn bag, 4" x 7.5" x 4.25". Right: white bag with clear cut lid and handle, Nelson Original. 4" x 8" x 3.5". $325-375 ea. *Courtesy of Dianne Rosenberg.*

Grey with clear cut lid and handle. Nelson Originals. 4.5" x 7" x 3.5". $350-375 *Courtesy of Susann Spilkin.*

This bag reminds one of a birdcage. The rhinestone trim really jazzes the bag with its matching purse. Made by Weisner. 5.5" x 5.5" x 3.5". $550-600 *Courtesy of Susann Spilkin.*

Black plastic bag with green ring handle made by Koret exclusively for the May Shoe Co. Charleston, W. VA. 9.5" (with handle) x 7.5" x 3". $500-575 *Courtesy of Susann Spilkin.*

Two plastic bags. Left: grey sparkle and pearl color plastic with clear cut lid and handle; unmarked; 8.75" x 4.25". $275-350 Right: reddish brown plastic with clear cut lid; Nelson Originals. 9.25" x 3.75". $275-325 *Courtesy of Radio Times.*

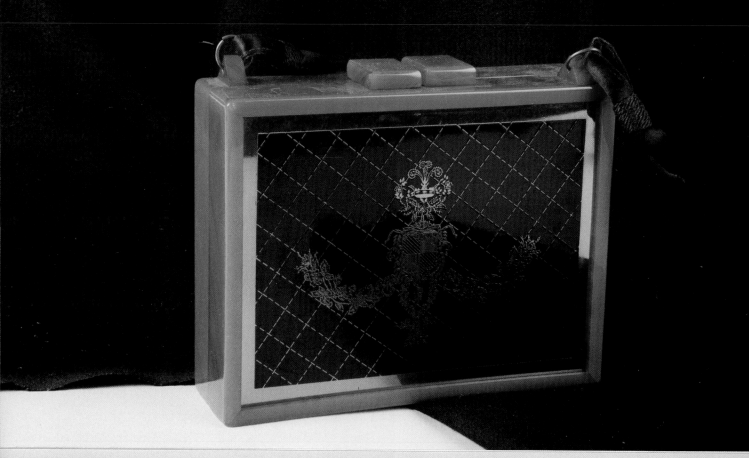

Above:
Brown plastic box with metal front and back displaying coats of arms. A brown silk handle is attached. Made by Vanity Fashions, New York. 7" x 5.5". $550-600 *Courtesy of Kuku Antiques.*

Below:
Pierced metal body elaborates the clear sides and dark lid with handle. Marked "Toro Di St., NYC." 8.25" x 3.5". $475-525 *Courtesy of Radio Times.*

Unusual clutch bag which could be taken for a strange cigar box. Marked "Toro, NYC." 2" x 8" x 4". $285-350 *Courtesy of Susann Spilkin.*

Black calf and brown plastic drum shape bag, 66 Berger Bags. 6" x 2". $475-500 *Courtesy of Rover and Lorber, NYC.*

Dark brown octagonal plastic handbag with lighter brown decorative plastic lid and brass clasp, marked Presto Lock Co. 7" x 4.5". $350-375 *Courtesy of Kuku Antiques.*

Dark brown bag decorated with gold rhinestones by Lewis. 3.25" x 6.25" x 3.5". $475-500 *Courtesy of Susann Spilkin.*

The same bag in black with rhinestones by Lewis. $475-500 *Courtesy of Dianne Rosenberg.*

Chartreuse bag with a clear lid. Yoniami. 8.25" x 5.25". $450-475 *Courtesy of Radio Times.*

Chapter 13
Unmarked Bags

Many bags have lost their tags or the tags have faded off, therefore many of these bags could be designer-made. As you will see when looking through them, many are unique and delightful.

Left: grey with gold threads angled sides, and a clear cut lid. 5" x 7" x 3.5". Right: curved edges, 4" x 8" x 4". $350-425 ea. *Courtesy of Susann Spilkin.*

Gold speckled plastic bag with matching accessories, unmarked. $275-325 *Courtesy of Anne Hopkin.*

Clear cylindrical shaped plastic trimmed with rhinestones sitting on four feet. 6.5" x 5". $400-475 *Courtesy of Peggy Osbourne.*

The glitter under this plastic makes for an interesting bag. Rhinestones decorate the top. Unmarked, 4" x 8" x 3.5". $400-475 *Courtesy of Susann Spilkin.*

Reddish-tortoise color with clear handle and lid, maker unknown. 5" x 10" x 5". $350-375 *Courtesy of Susann Spilkin.*

A rectangular plastic bag framed with metal. Similar to a Tyrolean bag. $325-350 *Courtesy of Anne Hopkin.*

All clear cut plastic bag of a narrow design. $275-350 *Courtesy of Anne Hopkin.*

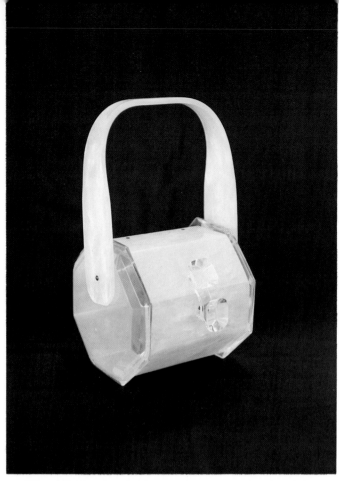

Grey with clear sides, maker uncertain. 5" x 6.5" x 4.5". $425-450 *Courtesy of Dianne Rosenberg.*

White marbled plastic bag with clear trim. Octagonal drum shape on its side. 5" h. $400-425 *Courtesy of Rover and Lorber, NYC.*

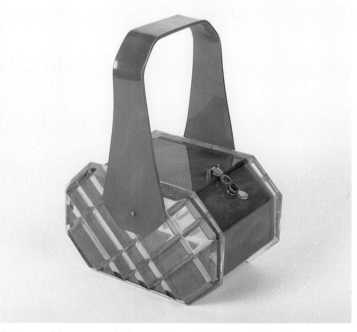

Octagonal brown and clear yellow plastic bag. 7" x 3". $425-450 *Courtesy of Kuku Antiques.*

Grey with gold threads and unusual raised "shoulders". 4" x 9" x 4.5". $375-400 *Courtesy of Susann Spilkin.*

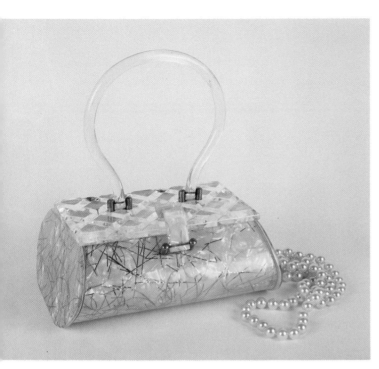

Pink bag with gold threads, maker uncertain. 3" x 7" x 4". $275-350 *Courtesy of Dianne Rosenberg.*

Pale grey bag with an unusual "bullet" top. 5" h. x 7.25" w. x 4" d. $450-475 *Courtesy of Susann Spilkin.*

Two bags of greenish-grey marbled plastic, makers uncertain. Left: 4" x 12" x 3". Right: 4" x 8" x 4". $275-350 ea. *Courtesy of Dianne Rosenberg.*

Grey bag with gold threads, maker uncertain. 4" x 5.5" x 3.5". $275-350 *Courtesy of Susann Spilkin.*

A striped bag with gold filigree on top and small post feet, maker uncertain. 3.5" x 8.5" x 4". $275-350 *Courtesy of Susann Spilkin.*

A rare and patriotic bag especially appropriate in the '50s, maker uncertain. 4" x 7.5" x 3.5". $475-500 due to unusual colors. *Courtesy of Susann Spilkin.*

A tall tortoise color bag with a half circle inset of filigree decorating the front. 9" x 8" x 3.5". $400-425 *Courtesy of Susann Spilkin.*

A grey, burl-like colored plastic. The curves of the handles match the curves of the bag with silver filigree on the flap of the lid. 6.5" x 6.5" x 3.5". $375-425 *Courtesy of Dianne Rosenberg.*

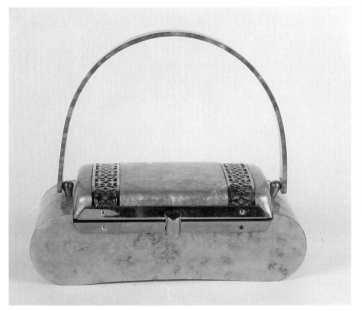

This peach colored bag could be perfect with just the right dress! The metal trim adds some seriousness. Maker unknown. 3" x 8.75" x 3.75". $425-450 *Courtesy of Dianne Rosenberg.*

The right necklace to go with this tortoise colored bag, maker unknown. 4" x 8.25" x 4.25". $275-325 *Courtesy of Dianne Rosenberg.*

Stainless steel and black plastic decorated with rhinestones. Unique shape, maker unknown. 4" x 7" x 6". $450-475 *Courtesy of Dianne Rosenberg.*

A brown swirled plastic with a heavy, amber, carved lid, maker unknown. 4.75" x 8" x 3.75". $275-325 *Courtesy of Susann Spilkin.*

Two orange bags with silver filigree trim. Left: the trapezoid shape was very common, maker unknown. 4" x 9" x 3.5". Right: maker unknown, 3.5" x 7" x 4.75". $300-350 ea. *Courtesy of Susann Spilkin.*

Black and clear cut plastic, maker unknown. 4.5" x 6.5" x 4.5". $375-400 *Courtesy of Susann Spilkin.*

Tall, clear plastic bag, maker unknown. 9" x 8.25" x 3.5". $425-450 *Courtesy of Susann Spilkin.*

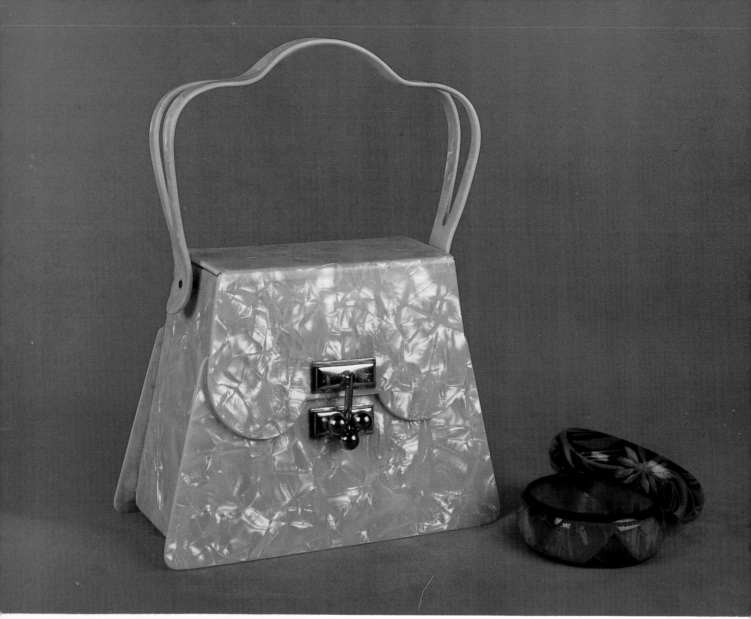

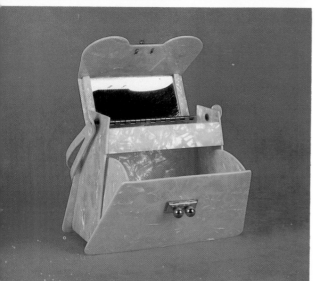

Yellowish-ivory bag with a split handle, maker
unknown. This bag opens on top and in front
as shown. 6" x 7" x 3.5". $400-450 *Courtesy of
Dianne Rosenberg.*

Interesting black plastic with three gold strips of trim, very modern looking, maker unknown. 4.5" x 8" x 3.5". $400-425 *Courtesy of Susann Spilkin.*

Decorative gold filigree diamonds sit in this unusually shaped bag, maker unknown. 5" x 6.75" x 7". $400-425 *Courtesy of Dianne Rosenberg.*

Left: the inside holds unusual compartments separated by clear plastic walls. Possibly by Herb Venzer. 6.75" x 6.75" x 3.75". Right: tortoise color with amber lid, maker unknown. 3.75" x 8.75" x 4.25". $375-400 ea. *Courtesy of Dianne Rosenberg.*

Yellow tortoise color with reverse
carved lid, maker unknown. 5.5" x
6.5" x 4.5". $375-425 *Courtesy of
Dianne Rosenberg.*

Marbled brown with gold threads and a three band handle, maker unknown. 4" x 10.5" x 3". $375-400 *Courtesy of Susann Spilkin.*

The typical trapezoid shape, maker unknown. 4" x 10" x 3.5". $275-350 *Courtesy of Dianne Rosenberg.*

Pink marble plastic handbag with a clear decorative handle. 5" x 8". $400-425 *Courtesy of Radio Times.*

Pail-shaped clear plastic with gold threads and speckles. The two buckles on the front left give interesting detail, maker unknown. 8" x 8" x 4.5". $375-425 *Courtesy of Susann Spilkin.*

Brown plastic with an elaborate sequined border on each side. 8.25" x 4". $400-450 *Courtesy of Radio Times.*

Elliptical-shaped grey plastic bag. $375-425 *Courtesy of Kuku Antiques.*

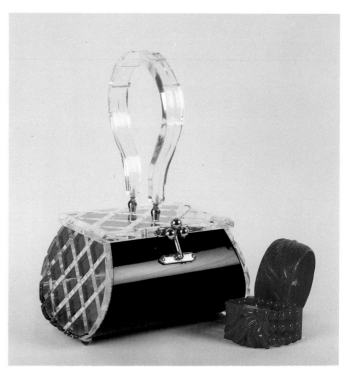

Grey plastic bag with clear cut lid. $350-375 *Courtesy of Radio Times.*

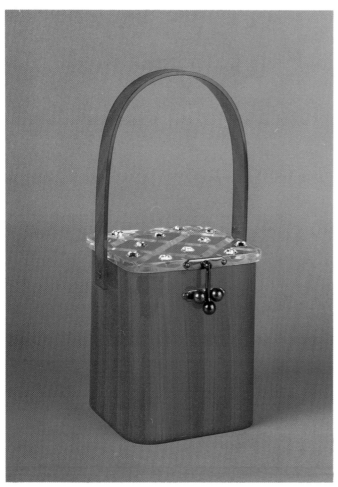

Plastic bag of brown vertical stripes with clear lid decorated with rhinestones. 5.75" x 5". $400-450 *Courtesy of Radio Times.*

Hatbox style plastic bag. 9" x 8". $400-425 *Courtesy of Radio Times.*

Interesting threaded plastic. $375-400 *Courtesy of Route 66.*

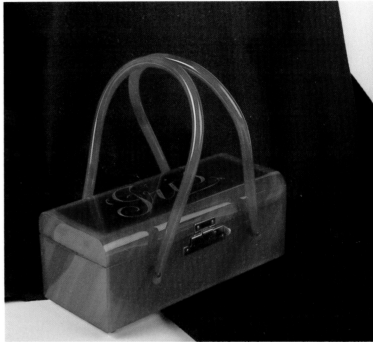

Brown plastic bag, tortoise color, with "Iris" engraved on the top. Sliding clasp in front and two handles, maker unknown. 8.5" x 3.5". $275-300 *Courtesy of Kuku Antiques.*

Light brown plastic bag with curves. 8.5" x 3.75". $375-400 *Courtesy of Kuku Antiques.*

Brown tortoise shell colored bag with single handle, maker unknown. 8.75" x 3.25". $300-350 *Courtesy of Kuku Antiques.*

All-clear cut plastic which gives the semblance of cut glass, maker unknown. 9.25" x 4.25". $375-425 *Courtesy of Radio Times.*

White marbled plastic, maker unknown. $275-325 *Courtesy of Radio Times.*

Pearl colored plastic bag with pierced metal trim. 7.75" x 3.5". $350-400 *Courtesy of Radio Times.*

Pink speckled plastic bag with clear handle, maker unknown. 7.5" x 3". $350-375 *Courtesy of Radio Times.*

Left, pink basket weave with cut clear lid, maker unknown, 8.75" x 3.5". Right: trapezoid with white lid and handle. Gold flowers with sparkles decorate the front of the bag, maker unknown. 9.25" x 3.5". $300-350 ea. *Courtesy of Route 66.*

Grey marble plastic handbag with scalloped ends, maker unknown. 4.5" x 9". $375-400 *Courtesy of Radio Times.*

Gold cylinder shaped bag with cut clear handle and sides, maker unknown. 6.5" x 5". $400-450 *Courtesy of Kuku Antiques.*

White pearled plastic bag with attractive clear plastic cut lid. Resembles a Charles Kahn design but is unmarked. $275-350 *Courtesy of Kuku Antiques.*

White marbled plastic drum shaped bag with spiral. 6.25". $425-450 *Courtesy of Rover and Lorber, NYC.*

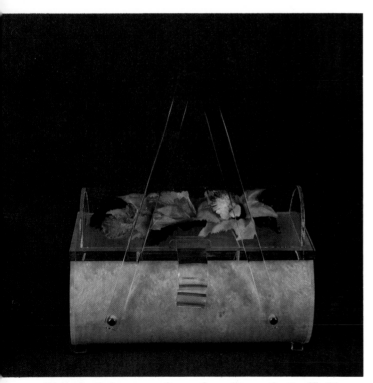

This plastic bag was often referred to as the "coffin" bag resembling a coffin laid out with flowers. Possibly by Harry Litwin. 5" x 7.5" x 4.75". $450-475 *Courtesy of Dianne Rosenberg.*

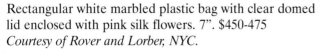

Rectangular white marbled plastic bag with clear domed lid enclosed with pink silk flowers. 7". $450-475 *Courtesy of Rover and Lorber, NYC.*

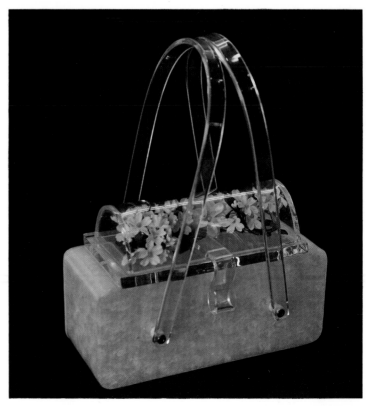

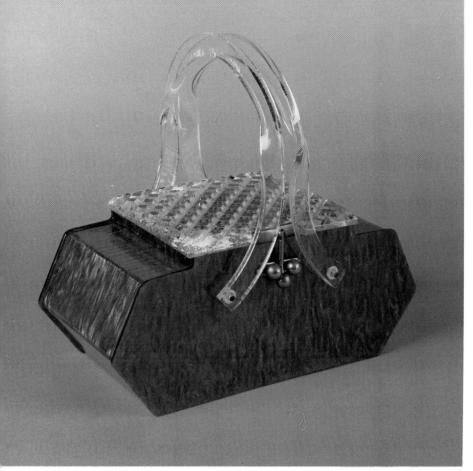

Grey basket weave bag of plastic with clear cut lid. 8.25" x 3.75". $325-350 *Courtesy of Radio Times.*

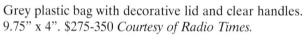

Grey plastic bag with decorative lid and clear handles. 9.75" x 4". $275-350 *Courtesy of Radio Times.*

Black plastic with silver sparkles and a clear handle. 10" x 4". $275-325 Light brown plastic bag with clear lid with insets. 6.75" x 5.5". $325-350 *Courtesy of Radio Times.*

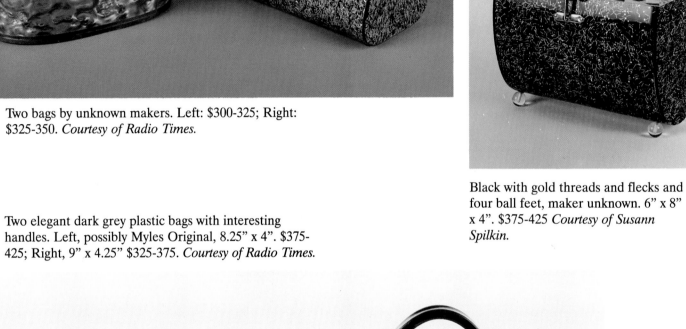

Two bags by unknown makers. Left: $300-325; Right: $325-350. *Courtesy of Radio Times.*

Two elegant dark grey plastic bags with interesting handles. Left, possibly Myles Original, 8.25" x 4". $375-425; Right, 9" x 4.25" $325-375. *Courtesy of Radio Times.*

Black with gold threads and flecks and four ball feet, maker unknown. 6" x 8" x 4". $375-425 *Courtesy of Susann Spilkin.*

Grey plastic bag with rhinestone border in front and around clasp. 8.5" x 5.25". $375-425 *Courtesy of Radio Times.*

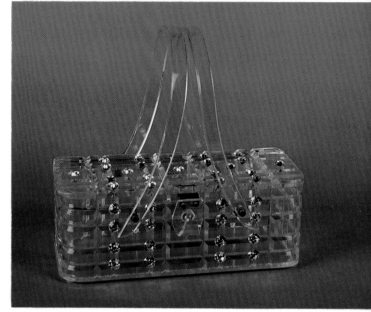

Clear cut with rhinestones. Unknown maker for Bergdorf Goodman. 3.5" x 9" x 4". $375-425 *Courtesy of Susann Spilkin.*

This bag almost looks like cut glass, maker unknown. 4" x 9" x 4". $325-375 *Courtesy of Susann Spilkin.*

Striped tortoise shell color with metal work on the lid. Maker unknown. 4" x 9" x 3". $300-350 *Courtesy of Susann Spilkin.*

Dark tortoise color and clear white bag of the same shape. 8.75" x 4.25" x 4.25". $425-475 ea. *Courtesy of Susann Spilkin.*

Very rare grey marbleized bag of a triangular shape. The side openings are covered with a metal decoration. Maker unknown. 6" x 8" x 3.5". $475-550 *Courtesy of Susann Spilkin.*

White bag, unknown maker. 4" x 8" x 4". $275-325
Courtesy of Susann Spilkin.

Interesting dark blue marbleized plastic, maker unknown.
8.5" x 3.75" x 3.5". $300-325 *Courtesy of Susann Spilkin.*

Grey marbleized bag with inset of grey encircled with
rhinestones on the lid. Maker unknown. 4" x 7.5" x 4".
$375-450 *Courtesy of Susann Spilkin.*

Cute pink bag with the gold confetti threads throughout.
7" x 4" x 4". $375-425 *Courtesy of Susann Spilkin.*

Brown bag with gold glitter and clear lid, maker unknown. 3.5" x 8" x 5". $300-325 *Courtesy of Susann Spilkin.*

Metal accordion style bag, maker unknown. 5" x 8.5" x 4.5". $250-275 *Courtesy of Dianne Rosenberg.*

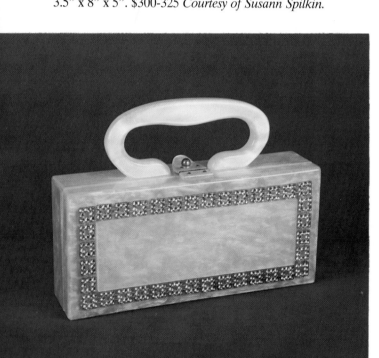

White rectangular bag with decorative trim, maker unknown. 4" x 8" x 2". $375-425 *Courtesy of Dianne Rosenberg.*

All clear bag decorated to appear as lace. Maker unknown. 3.5" x 8.5" x 4". $375-400 *Courtesy of Susann Spilkin.*

Fancy plastic covered with rhinestones. Maker unknown.
4.5" x 5" x 3.5". $475-500 *Courtesy of Susann Spilkin.*

Interesting contrast of black with gold threads, maker
unknown. 4.5" x 7" x 4". $350-385 *Courtesy of Dianne
Rosenberg.*

An elegant upright bag perfect for the evening. $300-350
Courtesy of Anne Hopkin.

Basketweave plastic with gold speckles. Maker unknown.
4" x 7" x 5". $375-400 *Courtesy of Dianne Rosenberg.*

Grey swirled plastic with decorative gemstone clasp. 4.75" x 10" x 5". $350-375 *Courtesy of Dianne Rosenberg.*

A hat box bag. Maker unknown. 8.5" x 9.5" x 4". $350-385 *Courtesy of Dianne Rosenberg.*

A unique handle that sits sideways. 4" x 8" x 4". $325-350 *Courtesy of Dianne Rosenberg.*

Definitely a party bag—creme with colored confetti. 5" x 8.5" x 3.5". $350-385 *Courtesy of Dianne Rosenberg.*

Brown bag with slit handles at bottom. Maker unknown. 4" x 7" x 4.75". $325-385 *Courtesy of Dianne Rosenberg.*

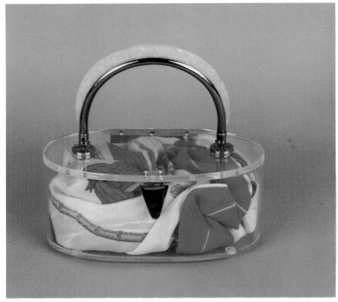

Clear Lucite purse, maker unknown. $275-300 *Courtesy of Steppin' Out.*

Plastic handbag with brown tortoise-patterned body and a clear, brilliant cut, hinged lid, 9" x 5". $325-375 *Courtesy of Piacente, Tarrytown, NY.*

Grey bag with cut pattern on lid and front, maker unknown. 6" x 7" x 4". $300-325 *Courtesy of Susann Spilkin.*

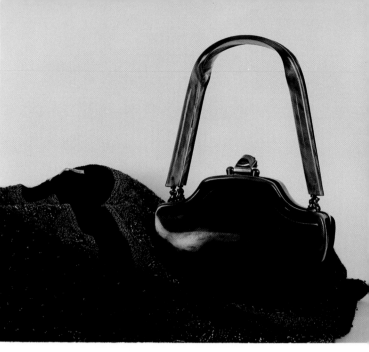

Clear bag decorated to resemble black and gold lace, maker unknown. 4.25" x 7" x 4.5". $400-450 *Courtesy of Dianne Rosenberg.*

Brown tortoise color bag resembling a design by Llewellyn, not marked however. 5.5" x 7" x 2.5". $300-325 *Courtesy of Susann Spilkin.*

Three clear Lucite purses, unmarked. $275-325 ea. *Courtesy of Steppin' Out.*

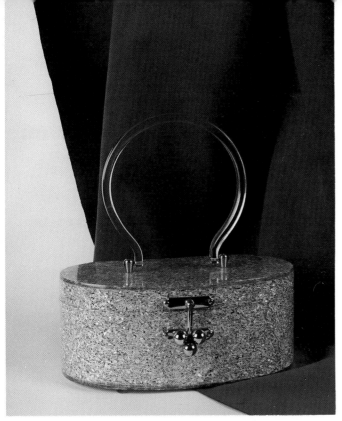

This unmarked bag displays unique insertions in the plastic, mirror on the inside lid. 3" x 7". $400-425 *Courtesy of Susann Spilkin.*

Another tortoise shell color with rhinestones decorating the lid, maker unknown. 6" x 6.75" x 4". $450-475 *Courtesy of Dianne Rosenberg.*

Light tortoise shell color with metal trim and metal buckle. 4" x 6" x 3.75". $400-425 *Courtesy of Dianne Rosenberg.*

This bag resembles a
Majestic but is unmarked.
6" x 5". $275-350 *Courtesy of
Dianne Rosenberg.*

Two clear plastic bags
decorated with rhinestones.
Makers unknown. $450-500
ea. *Courtesy of Dianne
Rosenberg.*

A fun bag with golden stars as inserts,
maker unknown. 5" x 7" x 3.75". $325-375
Courtesy of Dianne Rosenberg.

Clear bag with two rows of rhinestones
decorating the top and bottom of the bag,
maker unknown. 8.5" x 5.75" x 3.25".
$375-400 *Courtesy of Susann Spilkin.*

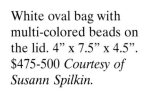

White oval bag with multi-colored beads on the lid. 4" x 7.5" x 4.5". $475-500 *Courtesy of Susann Spilkin.*

Metal mesh bag with plastic sides and handle. 4" x 6.5" x 1.5". $350-375 *Courtesy of Dianne Rosenberg.*

Black bag encrusted with rhinestones. 4.5" x 7.5". x 3.5". $450-500 *Courtesy of Susann Spilkin.*

Creamy whitish bag, marbleized with clear cut top. 4" x 10.5" x 3.5". $375-400 *Courtesy of Susann Spilkin.*

Grey with clear sides and lid. 6" x 7.5" x 4". $275-325 *Courtesy of Susann Spilkin.*

Tall grey bag with metal floral clasp bar. 10" x 8" x 3". $425-475 *Courtesy of Susann Spilkin.*

Gold with stars and threads on this cylindrical bag. 5" x 6.5" x 5". $375-425 *Courtesy of Susann Spilkin.*

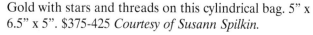

Grey bag trimmed with gold metal and black plastic lid and handle. $275-325 *Courtesy of Susann Spilkin.*

Tortoise color bag with a scooped back and rhinestone clasp. Maker unknown. 6.5" x 7.5" x 3.5". $350-375 *Courtesy of Susann Spilkin.*

Ethereal-looking bag with gold metal trim. Unmarked. $350-375 *Courtesy of Route 66.*

Grey marbleized plastic with gold threads throughout and clear handle. $300-325 *Courtesy of Radio Times.*

Two beaded bags of unknown makers. Each 7" x 8" x 4". $375-425 ea. *Courtesy of Dianne Rosenberg.*

Oval plastic bag with bronze colored beads and mechanical clasp. 5" x 8.5" x 4". $425-450 *Courtesy of Susann Spilkin.*

Fre-Mor box bags with beads decorating the body. Original owners of Fre-Mor later merged with Jewel Plastics Corp. to become Llewellyn Inc. Each bag 5" x 7" x 3". $450-475 *Courtesy of Susann Spilkin.*